Mastering the Morning

Mastering the Morning

Matthew Petchinsky

Mastering the Morning: How to Win the Day Before 8 AM
By: Matthew Petchinsky

Introduction: The Power of Mornings – Setting the Tone for Success

Mornings hold a unique power. They represent a fresh start, a chance to align your intentions with your actions, and an opportunity to set the tone for the rest of the day. A well-structured morning routine is not just a series of actions but a foundation upon which success is built. Whether you're striving for personal growth, professional excellence, or simply seeking to maximize your energy and focus, how you start your morning can be the difference between a day of fulfillment and one of missed opportunities.

Why Mornings Set the Tone for Success

The morning is the most precious and undisturbed part of the day, offering a quiet reprieve before the demands of life take over. This window of time is when your mind is most receptive, your energy levels are naturally at their peak, and the decisions you make are least influenced by external distractions. By intentionally designing your mornings, you set yourself up for clarity, focus, and momentum that carries throughout the day.

1. Establishing a Positive Mindset:

Mornings are a clean slate. The thoughts and actions you embrace during these early hours shape your mental and emotional state. Whether it's practicing gratitude, meditating, or journaling, these practices anchor you in positivity and empower you to face challenges with resilience.

2. Building Momentum:

Newton's first law tells us that an object in motion stays in motion. Similarly, a productive morning routine creates momentum that drives your productivity for the rest of the day. Accomplishing even small tasks in the morning—like making your bed, hydrating, or completing a quick workout—builds a sense of achievement that propels you forward.

3. Gaining Control:

In a world where distractions are constant, mornings are your opportunity to take control. Before emails flood your inbox or social media demands your attention, the early hours allow you to focus solely on what truly matters. This sense of control fosters confidence, reduces stress, and helps you approach the day with clarity.

4. Unlocking Creativity and Problem-Solving:

Studies have shown that the brain is most creative and resourceful shortly after waking. Taking advantage of this heightened state—through brainstorming, writing, or planning—can lead to breakthroughs and innovative solutions that might not come as easily later in the day.

How to Develop Your Ultimate Routine

Creating your ultimate morning routine isn't about replicating someone else's habits. Instead, it's about crafting a personalized set of rituals that align with your goals, values, and lifestyle. Here's how you can build a transformative routine tailored to your unique needs:

1. Start with a Clear Intention:

Begin by asking yourself what you want to achieve with your mornings. Are you seeking more energy? Greater focus? Improved health? Understanding your "why" provides a sense of purpose that keeps you consistent.

2. Optimize Your Wake-Up Time:

The time you wake up should support your goals while respecting your natural sleep cycle. Aim for a wake-up time that allows you to complete your routine without rushing. Consistency is key—waking up at the same time daily helps regulate your body clock and improves overall energy levels.

3. Prioritize Movement and Hydration:

Physical activity is a cornerstone of an effective morning routine. Whether it's yoga, stretching, or a brisk walk, movement wakes up your body and boosts endorphins, setting a positive tone. Pair this with proper hydration to kickstart your metabolism and rehydrate after hours of sleep.

4. Nourish Your Mind:

Feed your mind with practices that enhance focus and calm. Meditation, deep breathing exercises, or reading inspirational material can help you cultivate a sense of peace and clarity. Journaling your thoughts or goals can further refine your mental focus.

5. Align with Your Goals:

Dedicate time to activities that align with your long-term objectives. For instance, if you're working on a creative project, carve out quiet time to write. If professional growth is a priority, review your plans or tackle the most challenging task of the day.

6. Limit Screen Time:

Starting the day by scrolling through emails or social media can pull your focus away from your priorities. Instead, aim to spend your first hour offline, connecting with yourself rather than the outside world.

7. Reflect and Adjust:

No routine is perfect on the first try. Pay attention to what works and what doesn't. Regularly evaluate your morning habits and refine them to better serve your evolving goals and needs.

The Transformative Power of Morning Routines

Crafting and sticking to an effective morning routine is not about perfection; it's about progress. Over time, these small, consistent actions compound into lasting change. A well-curated morning sets the stage for a life of intentionality, productivity, and balance. Whether you're an early bird or a late riser, embracing the power of mornings allows you to seize control of your day—and, ultimately, your destiny.

Your mornings are the gateway to your best self. With intention, discipline, and a commitment to growth, you can create a routine that not only sets the tone for success but transforms your life in ways you never imagined. So, as you begin this journey, remember: the way you start your morning is the way you start your life. Make it count.

Chapter 1: Designing a Morning Ritual

A successful morning ritual is not a one-size-fits-all template; it's a deeply personal blueprint for starting your day with intention, focus, and purpose. Crafting a morning ritual that aligns with your goals and values takes thoughtful planning, experimentation, and a willingness to adapt as your needs evolve. This chapter guides you through the essential steps to design a morning ritual that empowers you to take charge of your day and, ultimately, your life.

Understanding the Importance of Ritual

A ritual is more than just a routine. While routines are habits performed regularly, rituals carry deeper meaning and purpose. Morning rituals set the stage for your day by creating a sense of mindfulness and alignment. When you consciously design your morning, you signal to yourself that your time, energy, and goals matter.

Key Benefits of a Morning Ritual:

- **Focus:** A ritual helps you prioritize tasks and reduce distractions.
- **Energy Management:** Morning habits like movement, hydration, and mindfulness rejuvenate your body and mind.
- **Emotional Stability:** Rituals foster calm and clarity, enabling you to face challenges with resilience.
- **Consistency:** Starting your day with familiar actions creates a rhythm that builds momentum for success.

Step 1: Assess Your Current Mornings

Before designing your ideal ritual, take a close look at how you currently spend your mornings. This reflection will help you identify unproductive habits and uncover opportunities for improvement.

Questions to Ask Yourself:

1. What is the first thing I do when I wake up?
2. How do I typically feel in the morning—rushed, tired, or energized?
3. Are there habits that drain my energy or waste time?
4. What are my most important priorities for the day, and when do I address them?
5. Do I feel in control of my mornings, or do they control me?

Step 2: Define Your Goals and Priorities

A meaningful morning ritual begins with clarity about what you want to achieve. Your goals will guide the structure and focus of your ritual.

Types of Goals to Consider:

1. **Physical:** Improve health, increase energy, or build strength.
2. **Mental:** Cultivate focus, learn new skills, or spark creativity.
3. **Emotional:** Foster gratitude, reduce stress, or strengthen relationships.
4. **Professional:** Boost productivity, plan priorities, or develop expertise.

Write down your goals and rank them by importance. This clarity ensures that your ritual is not only effective but also aligned with your values.

Step 3: Build the Core Components of Your Ritual

An effective morning ritual includes activities that address your physical, mental, and emotional well-being. Here are foundational elements to consider:

1. Wake-Up Routine:

Start your day with consistency. Set a wake-up time that aligns with your natural sleep cycles and stick to it. Use an alarm that feels gentle and uplifting, such as soothing music or a sunrise alarm clock.

2. Hydration:

After hours of sleep, your body is naturally dehydrated. Begin your day by drinking a glass of water to rehydrate, kickstart your metabolism, and boost energy.

3. Movement:

Physical activity, even if brief, wakes up your body and promotes blood flow. Options include yoga, stretching, walking, or a full workout. Tailor the intensity to your fitness level and preferences.

4. Mindfulness Practices:

Calm your mind and set intentions through meditation, deep breathing, or journaling. These practices reduce stress, enhance focus, and foster a positive mindset.

5. Nutrition:

Fuel your body with a balanced breakfast that includes proteins, healthy fats, and complex carbohydrates. Avoid sugary or heavily processed foods that can cause energy crashes.

6. Planning:

Take a few moments to review your day's agenda and prioritize key tasks. Use a planner, to-do list, or digital app to organize your schedule and set achievable goals.

Step 4: Personalize Your Ritual

Your morning ritual should reflect your unique lifestyle and aspirations. Avoid copying someone else's routine verbatim; instead, adapt ideas that resonate with you.

Personalization Tips:

- **Time Constraints:** If you have limited time, focus on high-impact activities like hydration, a 5-minute meditation, or a quick workout.
- **Interests:** Incorporate activities that you enjoy, such as listening to music, reading, or spending time with a pet.
- **Flexibility:** Allow room for variation to accommodate different days or moods. For example, your weekend ritual might be more relaxed than your weekday routine.

Step 5: Create an Ideal Environment

Your surroundings play a significant role in the success of your morning ritual. A cluttered or chaotic environment can disrupt focus and motivation.

Environment Optimization Tips:

- **Declutter:** Keep your space organized to promote a sense of calm and order.
- **Lighting:** Maximize natural light or use a daylight lamp to signal to your body that it's time to wake up.
- **Tools:** Have everything you need ready, such as a water bottle, journal, or workout gear.
- **Minimize Distractions:** Avoid checking your phone or engaging with digital screens until your ritual is complete.

Step 6: Start Small and Build Consistency

Starting a morning ritual can feel overwhelming, especially if you're trying to implement multiple changes at once. Begin with one or two activities and gradually add more as you build consistency.

Tips for Building Consistency:

1. Set realistic goals and timelines for each habit.
2. Track your progress using a journal or habit tracker.
3. Reward yourself for sticking to your routine, such as enjoying your favorite tea or a moment of quiet reflection.
4. Be patient. It takes time to establish a new ritual, but persistence pays off.

Step 7: Evaluate and Refine

Your morning ritual should evolve as your goals, needs, and circumstances change. Periodically review what's working and what isn't, and make adjustments accordingly.

Reflection Questions:

1. Do I feel more energized and focused after my ritual?
2. Are there activities that feel forced or unproductive?
3. How can I better align my ritual with my goals?

Conclusion

Designing a morning ritual is one of the most powerful steps you can take to elevate your daily life. It's a commitment to yourself—a declaration that your time, energy, and goals are worth prioritizing. By building a ritual that reflects your values and aspirations, you create a foundation for success that extends far beyond the early hours of the day. With consistency and intention, your morning ritual will become a transformative practice that empowers you to seize each day with purpose and enthusiasm.

Chapter 2: The Role of Sleep in Success

Sleep is often overlooked in discussions about success, yet it plays a critical role in achieving peak performance, maintaining physical health, and fostering emotional resilience. In this chapter, we delve into the science of sleep, its profound effects on the mind and body, and how optimizing your sleep habits can unlock your full potential.

The Science of Sleep

Sleep is far from a passive state; it is a complex and dynamic process essential for rejuvenation and repair. The body and brain undergo distinct physiological and neurological changes during sleep, divided into cycles of rapid eye movement (REM) and non-REM stages.

1. Non-REM Sleep:

This phase consists of three stages: light sleep, deep sleep, and very deep sleep. During this period:

- The body repairs tissues and builds muscle.
- The immune system strengthens.
- Blood pressure and heart rate decrease, promoting cardiovascular health.

2. REM Sleep:

This is the dream phase, where the brain processes emotions, consolidates memories, and enhances cognitive functions. REM sleep is critical for creativity, problem-solving, and emotional regulation.

A full sleep cycle lasts approximately 90 minutes, and adults typically need 4–6 cycles (7–9 hours) of quality sleep each night.

The Impact of Sleep on Success

Sleep influences nearly every aspect of life. From decision-making to emotional resilience, adequate sleep is a foundational pillar for success.

1. Enhanced Cognitive Performance:

Quality sleep improves focus, memory, and critical thinking. During sleep, the brain consolidates new information and clears out toxins that build up during the day, boosting mental clarity and problem-solving abilities.

2. Increased Productivity:

Well-rested individuals complete tasks more efficiently and with higher accuracy. Sleep deprivation, on the other hand, reduces productivity by impairing attention span, processing speed, and decision-making.

3. Emotional Regulation:

Sleep plays a crucial role in managing stress and maintaining emotional balance. A lack of sleep can amplify feelings of irritability, anxiety, and depression, hindering personal and professional relationships.

4. Physical Health and Energy:

Adequate sleep supports the body's recovery processes, strengthens the immune system, and regulates energy levels. Chronic sleep deprivation is linked to weight gain, cardiovascular issues, and a weakened immune response.

5. Creativity and Innovation:

Many groundbreaking ideas and creative solutions arise after a good night's sleep. REM sleep fosters abstract thinking and helps the brain make unique connections, fueling creativity and innovation.

The Consequences of Sleep Deprivation

Sleep deprivation doesn't just make you tired; it undermines your ability to function effectively. Chronic sleep deprivation can lead to:

- **Cognitive Decline:** Memory problems, difficulty concentrating, and slower reaction times.
- **Health Issues:** Increased risk of obesity, diabetes, heart disease, and stroke.
- **Emotional Instability:** Heightened stress, irritability, and difficulty managing emotions.
- **Burnout:** Persistent fatigue and reduced motivation can lead to burnout, negatively affecting your career and personal life.

The Sleep-Success Connection

The link between sleep and success is well-documented. Successful individuals often prioritize sleep as a key component of their routines. Famous leaders, athletes, and creatives alike have emphasized the importance of rest in achieving their goals.

Case Studies of Sleep-Savvy Achievers:

- **LeBron James:** The NBA star sleeps 8–10 hours a night and takes regular naps to maintain peak performance.
- **Jeff Bezos:** The Amazon founder prioritizes 8 hours of sleep, believing it enhances decision-making and productivity.
- **Arianna Huffington:** The media mogul champions the importance of sleep, crediting it with improving her health and career after a near-burnout experience.

Optimizing Your Sleep for Success

To harness the power of sleep, you must develop habits that promote restful and restorative sleep. Here's how to create an environment and routine that supports high-quality sleep:

1. Establish a Consistent Sleep Schedule:

Go to bed and wake up at the same time every day, even on weekends. Consistency helps regulate your body's internal clock (circadian rhythm) and improves sleep quality.

2. Create a Relaxing Bedtime Routine:

Wind down with calming activities such as reading, meditating, or taking a warm bath. Avoid stimulating activities like intense exercise or screen time close to bedtime.

3. Optimize Your Sleep Environment:

- **Darkness:** Use blackout curtains or a sleep mask to block out light.
- **Quiet:** Minimize noise with earplugs, a white noise machine, or soothing music.
- **Temperature:** Keep your bedroom cool, ideally between 60–67°F (15–19°C).
- **Comfort:** Invest in a quality mattress, pillows, and bedding to enhance comfort.

4. Limit Stimulants and Heavy Meals:

Avoid caffeine, nicotine, and large meals within a few hours of bedtime. These can disrupt your ability to fall and stay asleep.

5. Manage Stress and Anxiety:

Practice relaxation techniques such as deep breathing, journaling, or yoga to calm your mind and prepare for restful sleep.

6. Use Technology Wisely:

Blue light from screens can suppress melatonin production, delaying sleep onset. Use blue light filters, wear blue light-blocking glasses, or avoid screens for at least an hour before bed.

7. Monitor Sleep Quality:

Track your sleep with a journal or sleep-tracking device. Pay attention to patterns and make adjustments to improve your rest.

The Role of Naps in Success

Short naps (10–30 minutes) can boost energy and focus without disrupting nighttime sleep. Known as "power naps," they are particularly effective in combating midday fatigue.

Benefits of Napping:

- Improved alertness and reaction time.
- Enhanced mood and reduced stress.
- Increased cognitive performance and memory retention.

Balancing Sleep and Ambition

It's easy to fall into the trap of sacrificing sleep for work or personal pursuits, especially in high-pressure environments. However, this approach is counterproductive. Sleep isn't a luxury; it's a necessity. By prioritizing rest, you enhance your ability to perform at your best and sustain long-term success.

Conclusion

Sleep is not a barrier to productivity—it's a catalyst for success. By understanding its vital role and taking steps to optimize your sleep habits, you unlock the energy, focus, and resilience needed to achieve your goals. In the hustle and bustle of life, never forget: every successful day begins with a restful night. Embrace sleep as your ally, and watch it transform your path to success.

Chapter 3: Physical Energy Boosters

Energy is the currency of productivity, and maintaining high physical energy is essential for achieving success in any area of life. While mental clarity and emotional resilience play crucial roles, physical vitality forms the foundation for sustained performance. This chapter explores proven strategies to boost your physical energy, fuel your body, and create a lifestyle that supports peak performance.

The Importance of Physical Energy

Physical energy is more than just feeling awake; it's the ability to tackle tasks, maintain focus, and persevere throughout the day. High energy levels translate to increased productivity, resilience, and a greater sense of well-being. Conversely, low energy can lead to fatigue, irritability, and decreased performance.

Key Components of Physical Energy

To effectively boost physical energy, it's essential to focus on the following areas:

1. **Nutrition**
2. **Hydration**
3. **Exercise**
4. **Sleep Quality**
5. **Stress Management**

1.Nutrition: Fueling Your Body

Your body is like a high-performance engine that requires the right fuel to operate efficiently. Poor nutrition depletes energy, while a balanced diet sustains vitality.

Energy-Boosting Foods:

- **Complex Carbohydrates:** Whole grains, oats, and quinoa provide sustained energy by releasing glucose slowly into the bloodstream.
- **Healthy Fats:** Avocados, nuts, seeds, and olive oil support brain function and long-term energy.
- **Proteins:** Lean meats, eggs, tofu, and legumes are essential for muscle repair and energy production.
- **Fruits and Vegetables:** Rich in vitamins, minerals, and antioxidants, they combat fatigue and support overall health.

Foods to Avoid:

- **Refined Sugars:** While sugar provides a quick energy spike, it's followed by a crash that leaves you feeling tired.
- **Processed Foods:** High in unhealthy fats and sodium, these can lead to sluggishness.
- **Caffeine Overload:** Moderate caffeine can boost focus, but over-consumption can lead to dependency and energy crashes.

Practical Tips:

1. Eat small, balanced meals every 3–4 hours to maintain steady blood sugar levels.
2. Incorporate energy-boosting snacks like nuts, fruit, or yogurt.
3. Avoid skipping meals, especially breakfast, which kickstarts your metabolism.

2. Hydration: Staying Energized Through Water

Dehydration is a common but often overlooked cause of fatigue. Even mild dehydration can impair focus, physical performance, and mood.

How Much Water Do You Need?

- The standard recommendation is about 8 glasses (64 ounces) of water daily, but your needs may vary based on activity level, climate, and body weight.

Hydration Tips:

1. Start your day with a glass of water to rehydrate after sleep.
2. Keep a reusable water bottle handy and sip throughout the day.
3. Add flavor with slices of lemon, cucumber, or mint to make water more appealing.
4. Limit diuretics like caffeine and alcohol, which can contribute to dehydration.

3. Exercise: Generating Energy Through Movement

While it may seem counterintuitive, physical activity is one of the best ways to increase energy. Regular exercise enhances blood flow, oxygenates the body, and releases endorphins, improving both physical and mental stamina.

Types of Energy-Boosting Exercises:

1. **Cardiovascular Workouts:** Activities like running, cycling, or dancing increase heart rate and circulation, delivering oxygen and nutrients to cells.
2. **Strength Training:** Building muscle improves endurance and metabolism.
3. **Yoga and Stretching:** These practices reduce tension, improve flexibility, and boost energy through controlled breathing and mindful movement.
4. **Short Bursts of Activity:** High-Intensity Interval Training (HIIT) or quick 5-minute exercises can provide a significant energy boost.

Tips for Staying Active:

- Incorporate movement into your day with short walks, standing desks, or stretching breaks.
- Choose activities you enjoy to make exercise a habit.
- Aim for at least 150 minutes of moderate-intensity exercise weekly, as recommended by health experts.

4. Sleep Quality: The Foundation of Energy

While sleep was discussed in detail in the previous chapter, its role in sustaining physical energy cannot be overstated. Poor sleep reduces physical endurance, impairs metabolic function, and depletes energy reserves.

Quick Sleep Quality Tips:

- Stick to a consistent sleep schedule.
- Create a relaxing bedtime routine.
- Limit exposure to screens before bed.

5. Stress Management: Conserving Energy

Chronic stress drains energy by keeping your body in a state of heightened alertness. This constant "fight-or-flight" response can lead to physical and mental exhaustion.

Stress-Reducing Techniques:

1. **Breathing Exercises:** Deep, diaphragmatic breathing reduces stress and increases oxygen flow, boosting energy.
2. **Meditation:** Regular meditation calms the mind and conserves energy by reducing overthinking.
3. **Time in Nature:** Spending time outdoors can rejuvenate your energy and improve mental clarity.
4. **Time Management:** Prioritize tasks to reduce the overwhelm of juggling too many responsibilities.

Habits to Boost Energy Throughout the Day
Morning Energy Boosters:

- Start your day with light movement, such as stretching or yoga.
- Eat a nutritious breakfast that includes protein, complex carbs, and healthy fats.
- Expose yourself to natural light to signal your body that it's time to be alert.

Midday Energy Boosters:

- Avoid heavy lunches that can cause post-meal drowsiness.
- Take a brisk walk or engage in a 5-minute workout to refresh your body and mind.
- Stay hydrated and consider a healthy snack like nuts, fruit, or a smoothie.

Evening Energy Preservation:

- Avoid heavy meals and stimulants like caffeine close to bedtime.
- Wind down with calming activities to prepare for restful sleep.

Creating Your Energy-Boosting Plan

To consistently maintain high physical energy, develop a personalized plan tailored to your lifestyle and goals.

Step 1: Assess Your Current Energy Levels

- Identify patterns of fatigue or low energy.
- Note how factors like diet, sleep, and stress affect your energy.

Step 2: Set Clear Goals

- Decide what areas of your life need the most improvement (e.g., better nutrition, more exercise, improved sleep).

Step 3: Implement Small Changes

- Focus on one or two areas at a time, such as drinking more water or incorporating short bursts of exercise.

Step 4: Monitor and Adjust

- Regularly evaluate what's working and make changes as needed.

Conclusion

Your physical energy is the foundation of your success, fueling your ability to take on challenges, stay productive, and maintain resilience. By focusing on proper nutrition, hydration, regular exercise, quality sleep, and effective stress management, you can create a lifestyle that supports sustained energy and peak performance. Remember, small, consistent changes compound into significant results, empowering you to achieve your goals and live with vitality. Start today, and experience the transformative power of abundant energy in your life.

Chapter 4: Mental Preparation Techniques

Success is as much a mental game as it is physical. While physical energy provides the stamina to act, mental preparation sharpens focus, builds resilience, and enables you to navigate challenges with clarity and confidence. This chapter explores the art and science of mental preparation, offering practical techniques to cultivate a winning mindset and approach each day with purpose and determination.

The Importance of Mental Preparation

Mental preparation is about creating the psychological conditions necessary for success. Whether you're facing a high-stakes presentation, a demanding project, or simply the challenges of daily life, a prepared mind allows you to:

- **Focus on what matters most.**
- **Stay calm under pressure.**
- **Adapt to changing circumstances.**
- **Maintain confidence and resilience.**

By investing in mental preparation, you develop the ability to turn obstacles into opportunities and setbacks into stepping stones.

Key Elements of Mental Preparation

To effectively prepare your mind, focus on these core elements:

1. **Clarity:** Understanding your goals and priorities.
2. **Focus:** Minimizing distractions and concentrating on what matters.
3. **Resilience:** Cultivating emotional strength to handle adversity.
4. **Positivity:** Maintaining a constructive and optimistic outlook.

Techniques for Mental Preparation
1. Visualization: Picture Success

Visualization involves imagining yourself successfully completing a task or achieving a goal. This technique primes your brain for success by creating a mental blueprint of desired outcomes.

How to Practice Visualization:

1. **Find a Quiet Space:** Sit comfortably in a distraction-free environment.
2. **Close Your Eyes:** Visualize the scenario you want to succeed in, such as acing an interview or delivering a presentation.
3. **Engage All Senses:** Imagine the sights, sounds, feelings, and even smells associated with your success.
4. **Focus on Details:** Be as specific as possible. Picture your body language, tone of voice, and the reactions of others.
5. **Repeat Daily:** Practicing visualization consistently reinforces positive neural pathways.

Benefits of Visualization:

- Boosts confidence and reduces anxiety.
- Improves performance by mentally rehearsing success.
- Enhances focus by aligning your mind with your goals.

2. Goal Setting: Define Your Path

Clear goals provide a sense of direction and purpose. When your goals are well-defined, your mind can focus its energy on achieving them.

The SMART Goal Framework:

- **Specific:** Clearly define what you want to achieve.
- **Measurable:** Establish metrics to track progress.
- **Achievable:** Set realistic yet challenging goals.
- **Relevant:** Ensure your goals align with your larger aspirations.
- **Time-Bound:** Assign deadlines to create urgency and account-ability.

Daily Goal-Setting Tips:

- Start each morning by identifying your top three priorities.
- Break large goals into smaller, actionable steps.
- Reflect on your progress at the end of each day.

3. Affirmations: Build a Positive Mindset

Affirmations are positive statements that challenge self-doubt and reinforce confidence. By repeating affirmations, you reprogram your subconscious mind to focus on strengths rather than weaknesses.

How to Use Affirmations:

1. **Choose Affirmations That Resonate:** For example, "I am capable of overcoming any challenge" or "I approach my goals with focus and determination."
2. **Repeat Daily:** Say your affirmations aloud or write them down each morning.
3. **Believe in Your Words:** Pair affirmations with genuine belief to maximize their impact.

Why Affirmations Work:

- They replace negative self-talk with empowering thoughts.
- They boost self-esteem and motivation.
- They help you stay focused on your strengths.

4. Meditation and Mindfulness: Cultivate Presence

Meditation and mindfulness are powerful tools for reducing stress, improving focus, and enhancing emotional regulation. These practices train your mind to remain present, preventing distractions and negative thoughts from derailing your progress.

Mindfulness Techniques:

1. **Breath Awareness:** Focus on your breathing to anchor your mind in the present moment.
2. **Body Scans:** Gradually bring awareness to different parts of your body, releasing tension as you go.
3. **Gratitude Practice:** Reflect on things you're grateful for to shift your mindset toward positivity.

Meditation Tips for Beginners:

- Start with just 5–10 minutes a day.
- Use guided meditation apps or videos to help you get started.
- Be patient—mental clarity improves with consistent practice.

5. Mental Rehearsal: Practice in Your Mind

Mental rehearsal is a form of visualization that involves practicing tasks or scenarios in your mind before performing them. This technique is especially effective for high-pressure situations like speeches, interviews, or performances.

Steps for Mental Rehearsal:

1. Visualize the entire process, from start to finish.
2. Anticipate potential challenges and mentally practice overcoming them.
3. Focus on the feeling of success to reinforce confidence.

6. Journaling: Clarify Your Thoughts

Journaling is a powerful way to process emotions, gain clarity, and track progress. Writing helps you organize your thoughts and reflect on your goals, challenges, and achievements.

Types of Journaling:

- **Gratitude Journals:** List things you're grateful for each day to foster positivity.
- **Goal Journals:** Write about your short- and long-term goals.
- **Reflection Journals:** Analyze your successes, failures, and lessons learned.

Tips for Effective Journaling:

- Write consistently, even if only for a few minutes a day.
- Be honest and nonjudgmental in your writing.
- Review past entries to track growth and identify patterns.

7. Mental Priming: Set Your Intentions

Mental priming involves preparing your mind to perform at its best. This can include setting intentions, visualizing outcomes, or engaging in rituals that signal readiness.

Examples of Mental Priming:

- Listening to motivational music or speeches before starting work.
- Reciting a personal mantra to boost confidence.
- Reviewing your goals and action plan for the day.

8. Building Resilience: Strengthen Your Mind

Resilience is the ability to bounce back from setbacks and adapt to challenges. Building mental resilience ensures you stay focused and determined, even when facing adversity.

Strategies for Building Resilience:

1. **Practice Self-Compassion:** Treat yourself with kindness and understanding, especially after mistakes.
2. **Reframe Challenges:** View obstacles as opportunities for growth.
3. **Develop a Support System:** Surround yourself with people who inspire and encourage you.

Creating a Mental Preparation Plan

To consistently prepare your mind for success, create a personalized mental preparation plan:

Step 1: Identify Your Goals

- What do you want to achieve mentally (e.g., improved focus, reduced stress)?

Step 2: Choose Techniques That Work for You

- Select 2–3 techniques from this chapter that resonate most with your needs.

Step 3: Schedule Regular Practice

- Dedicate time each day for mental preparation, whether through journaling, meditation, or visualization.

Step 4: Reflect and Adjust

- Regularly evaluate your progress and adjust your techniques as needed.

Conclusion

Mental preparation is a powerful tool that sets the stage for success. By integrating techniques like visualization, affirmations, mindfulness, and journaling into your daily routine, you can cultivate focus, resilience, and confidence. Remember, success begins in the mind. The more you invest in preparing your mental landscape, the more equipped you'll be to conquer challenges, seize opportunities, and achieve your greatest aspirations. Let this chapter be your guide to mastering the mental edge and unlocking the limitless potential of your mind.

Chapter 5: Making Your Morning Routine Stick

Creating a morning routine is an empowering step, but the real challenge lies in sustaining it. Consistency transforms your routine from a fleeting experiment into a powerful habit that anchors your day in success. In this chapter, we'll explore strategies for making your morning routine stick, overcoming common obstacles, and maintaining motivation to ensure your morning habits become a permanent part of your lifestyle.

Why Consistency Matters

A consistent morning routine offers more than just a productive start to the day; it fosters long-term benefits by:

1. **Building Momentum:** Regularity in your mornings sets the tone for consistency in other areas of your life.
2. **Reinforcing Habits:** Repetition strengthens neural pathways, making your routine automatic over time.
3. **Reducing Decision Fatigue:** Following a set routine minimizes the need for daily decision-making, freeing up mental energy for other tasks.
4. **Fostering Discipline:** Sticking to a routine enhances your ability to remain disciplined and committed in other areas of life.

The Science of Habit Formation

Habits are formed through a cycle of three components:

1. **Cue:** A trigger that initiates the behavior (e.g., your alarm clock or the sight of your workout clothes).
2. **Routine:** The behavior itself (e.g., exercising, journaling, or meditating).
3. **Reward:** The benefit or satisfaction derived from the behavior (e.g., feeling energized or accomplished).

By intentionally shaping each of these components, you can create habits that are more likely to stick.

Step 1: Start Small

The key to long-term success is starting with manageable changes. Overwhelming yourself with an elaborate routine can lead to burnout or abandonment.

Tips for Starting Small:

- Choose 1–2 simple actions to include in your routine initially, such as drinking water or stretching.
- Keep the time commitment minimal, such as a 5-minute meditation or a quick journal entry.
- Gradually add more elements as the initial habits become second nature.

Step 2: Anchor Your Routine to Existing Habits

Pairing a new habit with an existing one creates a natural connection and makes the new habit easier to remember.

Examples of Anchoring:

- Drink a glass of water immediately after brushing your teeth.
- Write in your journal while your coffee brews.
- Do a quick stretch before stepping into the shower.

By linking your new habits to activities you already perform daily, you build a seamless transition into your morning routine.

Step 3: Plan Ahead

Preparation is crucial for minimizing friction and ensuring your routine runs smoothly.

Ways to Plan Ahead:

1. **Prepare Your Environment:** Lay out your workout clothes, set up your journal, or prepare breakfast ingredients the night before.
2. **Set Alarms and Reminders:** Use alarms, calendar notifications, or habit-tracking apps to keep you on schedule.
3. **Anticipate Challenges:** Identify potential obstacles, such as feeling too tired or pressed for time, and plan solutions in advance.

Step 4: Create Accountability

Accountability helps reinforce your commitment to your routine. Knowing that someone else is aware of your goals can motivate you to follow through.

Accountability Strategies:

- **Find a Partner:** Share your goals with a friend or family member and check in with each other regularly.
- **Join a Community:** Participate in online forums, social media groups, or local meetups focused on personal development or productivity.
- **Track Your Progress:** Use a journal or app to log your routine. Visualizing your streak can inspire you to keep going.

Step 5: Embrace Rewards

Rewards reinforce the habit loop by creating a positive association with your routine. A reward doesn't need to be extravagant; it should simply feel satisfying.

Examples of Rewards:

- Enjoy a cup of your favorite tea after completing your routine.
- Spend a few moments reading a book or listening to music you love.
- Reflect on your accomplishments and acknowledge your progress.

Step 6: Overcome Common Obstacles

Sticking to a morning routine isn't without challenges. Here's how to address some common hurdles:

1. Lack of Time:

- Wake up just 10–15 minutes earlier and gradually extend your routine as you adapt.
- Combine activities (e.g., listen to a podcast while stretching).

2. Inconsistent Wake-Up Times:

- Set a consistent bedtime and wake-up time, even on weekends, to regulate your sleep cycle.
- Use an alarm that mimics natural light to make waking up easier.

3. Motivation Slumps:

- Remind yourself of your "why" by revisiting your goals.
- Keep your routine flexible and adjust it to keep it engaging.

4. Overwhelm:

- Focus on progress, not perfection. It's okay to have an off day; what matters is getting back on track.

Step 7: Adapt and Evolve

Your morning routine should grow with you. As your goals, priorities, and circumstances change, revisit your routine and make adjustments.

Questions to Ask When Evolving Your Routine:

- Are all elements of my routine still serving my goals?
- What activities feel most energizing or fulfilling?
- Are there new habits I'd like to incorporate?

Step 8: Cultivate a Growth Mindset

Success with your morning routine requires patience and a willingness to learn from setbacks. Cultivating a growth mindset helps you view challenges as opportunities for improvement rather than reasons to quit.

Growth Mindset Practices:

- **Celebrate Small Wins:** Acknowledge even minor achievements to build confidence.
- **Reframe Failures:** Treat missed days as learning experiences, not failures.
- **Stay Curious:** Experiment with different activities to find what works best for you.

Morning Routine Checklist

To help you implement and maintain your morning routine, use this checklist as a guide:

1. **Prepare the Night Before:**
   ◦ Lay out clothes and supplies.
   ◦ Plan your first task for the morning.
   ◦ Set your wake-up alarm.
2. **Set Your Intention:**
   ◦ Review your goals for the day.
   ◦ Visualize success and commit to your routine.
3. **Start with Small Wins:**
   ◦ Drink a glass of water.
   ◦ Make your bed or complete a quick, easy task.
4. **Incorporate Energizing Activities:**
   ◦ Include movement, mindfulness, and goal setting.
   ◦ Keep the activities short and enjoyable.
5. **Track and Reflect:**
   ◦ Log your routine in a journal or app.
   ◦ Reflect on what's working and adjust as needed.
6. **Reward Yourself:**
   ◦ Celebrate your efforts with small rewards.

Conclusion

Building a consistent morning routine requires intention, effort, and adaptability, but the rewards are immeasurable. By starting small, planning ahead, and staying committed, you can transform your mornings into a time of focus, energy, and success. Remember, the key to lasting change lies not in perfection but in persistence. Stay the course, and watch as your morning routine becomes the foundation of a more productive, fulfilling life.

Appendix A: Morning Planner Template

Having a structured morning planner is one of the most effective ways to stay consistent with your routine and ensure your mornings align with your goals. This appendix provides a comprehensive morning planner template to help you organize your activities, track progress, and optimize your mornings for productivity and success.

How to Use This Template

1. **Customize Your Planner:** Adjust the template to suit your goals, priorities, and lifestyle.
2. **Plan the Night Before:** Spend a few minutes in the evening filling out your morning planner. This reduces decision-making fatigue and helps you start your day with clarity.
3. **Reflect and Adjust:** At the end of each week, review your planner to identify what worked and what didn't. Use this insight to refine your routine.

Morning Planner Template
Personal Information (Optional)

- **Name:** _____
- **Date:** _____
- **Day of the Week:** _____

Section 1: Morning Goals
What are your top three priorities for the morning?
Section 2: Wake-Up Routine
What time will you wake up?

- Planned wake-up time: _____

Morning mantra or affirmation:
Initial activity upon waking (e.g., drink water, stretch):
Section 3: Energize Your Body
What activities will you do to boost your physical energy?

- Movement/Exercise:

_____

- Duration: _____
- Hydration Plan (e.g., drink 16 oz of water):

_____

Section 4: Mindfulness and Focus
What practices will you include to cultivate mental clarity and focus?

- Mindfulness Activity (e.g., meditation, journaling):
_____
- Duration: _____

Gratitude Practice:

- Three things I'm grateful for:

Section 5: Nourishment
What will you eat for breakfast to fuel your day?

- Planned   Meal:

_____

Snacks (if applicable):
Section 6: Productivity and Planning
What tasks or goals will you focus on during your morning productivity session?

- Task   1:

_____

- Task   2:

_____

- Task   3:

_____

Time allocated for planning your day:
Section 7: Personal Development
How will you invest in yourself during the morning?

- Activity   (e.g.,   reading,   learning   a   new   skill):
  _____

- Duration: _____

Section 8: Morning Reflection
Reflect on your morning routine:

- How did your morning go?

  _____

- What worked well?

  _____

- What could be improved tomorrow?

  _____

Weekly Review Section
Complete this section at the end of the week to assess your progress.

- **Successes this week:**

  _____

- **Challenges faced:**

  _____

- **Adjustments for next week:**

  _____

Printable Version

To make this template even more practical, print several copies and bind them into a personalized morning planner. You can also digitize the template using apps like Notion, Evernote, or Google Docs for easy access and tracking.

Final Thoughts

This Morning Planner Template is designed to help you take control of your mornings, prioritize your goals, and maintain consistency. Remember, the key to success lies in preparation and intentionality. Use this tool daily to unlock the power of your mornings and set the tone for a productive and fulfilling life.

Message from the Author:

I hope you enjoyed this book, I love astrology and knew there was not a book such as this out on the shelf. I love metaphysical items as well. Please check out my other books:

-Life of Government Benefits

-My life of Hell

-My life with Hydrocephalus

-Red Sky

-World Domination:Woman's rule

-World Domination:Woman's Rule 2: The War

-Life and Banishment of Apophis: book 1

-The Kidney Friendly Diet

-The Ultimate Hemp Cookbook

-Creating a Dispensary(legally)

-Cleanliness throughout life: the importance of showering from childhood to adulthood.

-Strong Roots: The Risks of Overcoddling children

-Hemp Horoscopes: Cosmic Insights and Earthly Healing

- Celestial Hemp Navigating the Zodiac: Through the Green Cosmos

-Astrological Hemp: Aligning The Stars with Earth's Ancient Herb

-The Astrological Guide to Hemp: Stars, Signs, and Sacred Leaves

-Green Growth: Innovative Marketing Strategies for your Hemp Products and Dispensary

-Cosmic Cannabis

-Astrological Munchies

-Henry The Hemp

-Zodiacal Roots: The Astrological Soul Of Hemp

- **Green Constellations: Intersection of Hemp and Zodiac**

-Hemp in The Houses: An astrological Adventure Through The Cannabis Galaxy

-Galactic Ganja Guide

Heavenly Hemp

Zodiac Leaves

Doctor Who Astrology

Cannastrology

Stellar Satvias and Cosmic Indicas

Celestial Cannabis: A Zodiac Journey

AstroHerbology: The Sky and The Soil: Volume 1

AstroHerbology:Celestial Cannabis:Volume 2

Cosmic Cannabis Cultivation

The Starry Guide to Herbal Harmony: Volume 1

The Starry Guide to Herbal Harmony: Cannabis Universe: Volume
2

Yugioh Astrology: Astrological Guide to Deck, Duels and more

Nightmare Mansion: Echoes of The Abyss

Nightmare Mansion 2: Legacy of Shadows

Nightmare Mansion 3: Shadows of the Forgotten

Nightmare Mansion 4: Echoes of the Damned

The Life and Banishment of Apophis: Book 2

Nightmare Mansion: Halls of Despair

Healing with Herb: Cannabis and Hydrocephalus

Planetary Pot: Aligning with Astrological Herbs: Volume 1

Fast Track to Freedom: 30 Days to Financial Independence Using AI, Assets, and Agile Hustles

Cosmic Hemp Pathways

How to Become Financially Free in 30 Days: 10,000 Paths to Prosperity

Zodiacal Herbage: Astrological Insights: Volume 1

Nightmare Mansion: Whispers in the Walls

The Daleks Invade Atlantis

Henry the hemp and Hydrocephalus

10X The Kidney Friendly Diet

Cannabis Universe: Adult coloring book

Hemp Astrology: The Healing Power of the Stars

Zodiacal Herbage: Astrological Insights: Cannabis Universe: Volume 2

<u>Planetary Pot: Aligning with Astrological Herbs: Cannabis Universes: Volume 2</u>

Doctor Who Meets the Replicators and SG-1: The Ultimate Battle for Survival

Nightmare Mansion: Curse of the Blood Moon

<u>The Celestial Stoner: A Guide to the Zodiac</u>

Cosmic Pleasures: Sex Toy Astrology for Every Sign

Hydrocephalus Astrology: Navigating the Stars and Healing Waters

Lapis and the Mischievous Chocolate Bar

Celestial Positions: Sexual Astrology for Every Sign

Apophis's Shadow Work Journal: : A Journey of Self-Discovery and Healing

Kinky Cosmos: Sexual Kink Astrology for Every Sign

Digital Cosmos: The Astrological Digimon Compendium

Stellar Seeds: The Cosmic Guide to Growing with Astrology

Apophis's Daily Gratitude Journal

Cat Astrology: Feline Mysteries of the Cosmos

The Cosmic Kama Sutra: An Astrological Guide to Sexual Positions

Unleash Your Potential: A Guided Journal Powered by AI Insights

Whispers of the Enchanted Grove

Cosmic Pleasures: An Astrological Guide to Sexual Kinks

369, 12 Manifestation Journal

Whisper of the nocturne journal(blank journal for writing or drawing)

The Boogey Book

Locked In Reflection: A Chastity Journey Through Locktober

Generating Wealth Quickly:

How to Generate $100,000 in 24 Hours

Star Magic: Harness the Power of the Universe

The Flatulence Chronicles: A Fart Journal for Self-Discovery

The Doctor and The Death Moth

Seize the Day: A Personal Seizure Tracking Journal

The Ultimate Boogeyman Safari: A Journey into the Boogie World and Beyond

Whispers of Samhain: 1,000 Spells of Love, Luck, and Lunar Magic: Samhain Spell Book

Apophis's guides:

Witch's Spellbook Crafting Guide for Halloween

Frost & Flame: The Enchanted Yule Grimoire of 1000 Winter Spells

The Ultimate Boogey Goo Guide & Spooky Activities for Halloween Fun

Harmony of the Scales: A Libra's Spellcraft for Balance and Beauty

The Enchanted Advent: 36 Days of Christmas Wonders

Nightmare Mansion: The Labyrinth of Screams

Harvest of Enchantment: 1,000 Spells of Gratitude, Love, and Fortune for Thanksgiving

The Boogey Chronicles: A Journal of Nightly Encounters and Shadowy Secrets

The 12 Days of Financial Freedom: A Step-by-Step Christmas Countdown to Transform Your Finances

Sigil of the Eternal Spiral Blank Journal

A Christmas Feast: Timeless Recipes for Every Meal

Holiday Stress-Free Solutions: A Survival Guide to Thriving During the Festive Season

Yu-Gi-Oh! Holiday Gifting Mastery: The Ultimate Guide for Fans and Newcomers Alike

Holiday Harmony: A Hydrocephalus Survival Guide for the Festive Season

Celestial Craft: The Witch's Almanac for 2025 – A Cosmic Guide to Manifestations, Moons, and Mystical Events

Doctor Who: The Toymaker's Winter Wonderland

Tulsa King Unveiled: A Thrilling Guide to Stallone's Mafia Masterpiece

Pendulum Craft: A Complete Guide to Crafting and Using Personalized Divination Tools

Nightmare Mansion: Santa's Eternal Eve

Starlight Noel: A Cosmic Journey through Christmas Mysteries

The Dark Architect: Unlocking the Blueprint of Existence

Surviving the Embrace: The Ultimate Guide to Encounters with The Hugging Molly

The Enchanted Codex: Secrets of the Craft for Witches, Wiccans, and Pagans

Harvest of Gratitude: A Complete Thanksgiving Guide

Yuletide Essentials: A Complete Guide to an Authentic and Magical Christmas

Celestial Smokes: A Cosmic Guide to Cigars and Astrology

Living in Balance: A Comprehensive Survival Guide to Thriving with Diabetes Insipidus

Cosmic Symbiosis: The Venom Zodiac Chronicles

The Cursed Paw of Ambition

Cosmic Symbiosis: The Astrological Venom Journal

Celestial Wonders Unfold: A Stargazer's Guide to the Cosmos (2024-2029)

The Ultimate Black Friday Prepper's Guide: Mastering Shopping Strategies and Savings

Cosmic Sales: The Astrological Guide to Black Friday Shopping
Legends of the Corn Mother and Other Harvest Myths
Whispers of the Harvest: The Corn Mother's Journal
The Evergreen Spellbook
The Doctor Meets the Boogeyman
The White Witch of Rose Hall's SpellBook
The Gingerbread Golem's Shadow: A Study in Sweet Darkness
The Gingerbread Golem Codex: An Academic Exploration of Sweet Myths
The Gingerbread Golem Grimoire: Sweet Magicks and Spells for the Festive Witch
The Curse of the Gingerbread Golem
10-minute Christmas Crafts for kids
Christmas Crisis Solutions: The Ultimate Last-Minute Survival Guide
Gingerbread Golem Recipes: Holiday Treats with a Magical Twist
The Infinite Key: Unlocking Mystical Secrets of the Ages
Enchanted Yule: A Wiccan and Pagan Guide to a Magical and Memorable Season
Dinosaurs of Power: Unlocking Ancient Magick
Astro-Dinos: The Cosmic Guide to Prehistoric Wisdom
Gallifrey's Yule Logs: A Festive Doctor Who Cookbook
The Dino Grimoire: Secrets of Prehistoric Magick
The Gift They Never Knew They Needed
The Gingerbread Golem's Culinary Alchemy: Enchanting Recipes for a Sweetly Dark Feast
A Time Lord Christmas: Holiday Adventures with the Doctor
Krampusproofing Your Home: Defensive Strategies for Yule
Silent Frights: A Collection of Christmas Creepypastas to Chill Your Bones
Santa Raptor's Jolly Carnage: A Dino-Claus Christmas Tale
Prehistoric Palettes: A Dino Wicca Coloring Journey
The Christmas Wishkeeper Chronicles

The Starlight Sleigh: A Holiday Journey
Elf Secrets: The True Magic of the North Pole
Candy Cane Conjurations
Cooking with Kids: Recipes Under 20 Minutes
Doctor Who: The TARDIS Confiscation
The Anxiety First Aid Kit: Quick Tools to Calm Your Mind
Frosty Whispers: A Winter's Tale
The Infinite Key: Unlocking the Secrets to Prosperity, Resilience, and Purpose
The Grasping Void: Why You'll Regret This Purchase
Astrology for Busy Bees: Star Signs Simplified
The Instant Focus Formula: Cut Through the Noise
The Secret Language of Colors: Unlocking the Emotional Codes
Sacred Fossil Chronicles: Blank Journal
The Christmas Cottage Miracle
Feeding Frenzy: Graboid-Inspired Recipes
Manifest in Minutes: The Quick Law of Attraction Guide
The Symbiote Chronicles: Doctor Who's Venomous Journey
Think Tiny, Grow Big: The Minimalist Mindset
The Energy Key: Unlocking Limitless Motivation
New Year, New Magic: Manifesting Your Best Year Yet
Unstoppable You: Mastering Confidence in Minutes
Infinite Energy: The Secret to Never Feeling Drained
Lightning Focus: Mastering the Art of Productivity in a Distracted World
Saturnalia Manifestation Magick: A Guide to Unlocking Abundance During the Solstice
Graboids and Garland: The Ultimate Tremors-Themed Christmas Guide
12 Nights of Holiday Magic
The Power of Pause: 60-Second Mindfulness Practices
The Quick Reset: How to Reclaim Your Life After Burnout
The Shadow Eater: A Tale of Despair and Survival

The Micro-Mastery Method: Transform Your Skills in Just Minutes a Day

Reclaiming Time: How to Live More by Doing Less

Chronovore: The Eternal Nexus

The Mind Reset: Unlocking Your Inner Peace in a Chaotic World

Confidence Code: Building Unshakable Self-Belief

Baby the Vampire Terrier

Baby the Vampire Terrier's Christmas Adventure

Celestial Streams: The Content Creator's Astrology Manual

The Wealth Whisperer: Unlocking Abundance with Everyday Actions

The Energy Equation: Maximize Your Output Without Burning Out

The Happiness Algorithm: Science-Backed Steps to Joyful Living

Stress-Free Success: Achieving Goals Without Anxiety

Mindful Wealth: The New Blueprint for Financial Freedom

The Festive Flavors of New Year: A Culinary Celebration

The Master's Gambit: Keys of Eternal Power

Shadowed Secrets: Groundhog Day Mysteries

Beneath the Burrow: Lessons from the Groundhog

Spring's Whispers: The Groundhog's Prediction

The Limitless Mindset: Unlock Your Untapped Potential

The Focus Funnel: How to Cut Through Chaos and Get Results

Bold Moves: Building Courage to Live on Your Terms

The Daily Shift: Simple Practices for Lasting Transformation

The Quarter-Life Reset: Thriving in Your 20s and 30s

The Art of Shadowplay: Building Your Own Personal Myth

The Eternal Loop: Finding Purpose in Repetition

Burrowing Wisdom: Life Lessons from the Groundhog

Shadow Work: A Groundhog Day Perspective

Love in Bloom: 5-Minute Romantic Gestures

The Shadowspell Codex: Secrets of Forbidden Magick

The Burnout Cure: Finding Balance in a Busy World

The Groundhog Prophecy: Unlocking Seasonal Secrets

Nog Tales: The Spirited History of Eggnog

Six More Weeks: Embracing Seasonal Transitions

The Lumivian Chronicles: Fragments of the Fifth Dimension

Money on Your Mind: A Beginner's Guide to Wealth

The Focus Fix: Breaking Through Distraction

January's Spirit Keepers: Mystical Protectors of the Cold

Creativity Unchained: Unlocking Your Wildest Ideas in 2025

Manifestation Mastery: 365 Days to Rewrite Your Reality

The Groundhog's Mirror: Reflecting on Change

The Weeping Angels' Christmas Curse

Burrowed in Time: A Groundhog Day Journey

Heartbeats: Poems to Share with Your Valentine

Dino Wicca: The Sacred Grimoire of Prehistoric Magick

Courage of the Pride: Finding Your Inner Roar

The Lion's Leap: Bold Moves for Big Results

Healthy Hustle: Achieving Without Overworking

Practical Manifesting: Turning Dreams into Reality in 2025

Jurassic Pharaohs: Unlocking the Magick of Ancient Egypt and Dino Wicca

The Happiness Equation: Small Changes for Big Joy

The Confidence Compass: Finding Your Inner Strength

Whispers in the Hollow: Tales of the Forgotten Beasts

Echoes from the Hollow: The Return of Forgotten Beasts

The Hollow Ascendant: The Rise of the Forgotten Beasts

The Relationship Reset: Building Better Connections

If you want solar for your home go here: https://www.harborso-lar.live/apophisenterprises/

Get Some Tarot cards: https://www.makeplayingcards.com/sell/ apophis-occult-shop

Get some shirts: https://www.bonfire.com/store/apophis-shirt-emporium/

Instagrams:
@apophis_enterprises,
@apophisbookemporium,
@apophisscardshop
Twitter: @apophisenterpr1
Tiktok:@apophisenterprise
Youtube: @sg1fan23477, @FiresideRetreatKingdom
Hive: @sg1fan23477
CheeLee: @SG1fan23477

Podcast: Apophis Chat Zone: https://open.spotify.com/show/
5zXbrCLEV2xzCp8ybrfHsk?si=fb4d4fdbdce44dec

Newsletter: https://apophiss-newsletter-27c897.beehiiv.com/

If you want to support me or see posts of other projects that I have come over to: **buymeacoffee.com/mpetchinskg**

I post there daily several times a day

Get your Dinowicca or Christmas themed digital products, especially Santa Raptor songs and other musics. Here: **https://sg1fan23477.gumroad.com**

Apophis Yuletide Digital has not only digital Christmas items, but it will have all things with Dinowicca as well as other Digital products.

www.ingramcontent.com/pod-product-compliance
Ingram Content Group UK Ltd.
Pitfield, Milton Keynes, MK11 3LW, UK
UKHW020518240125
454132UK00011B/283